Cooking with Monkey Productions Corp.
#205-251 Lawrence Ave.
Kelowna, British Columbia, V1Y6L2
Canada

Buck

Author: Dustin Cromarty
Illustrator: Yanet Zamudio Castro
Colourist: Omar Lara Cadó
Graphic Designer: Omar Lara Cado
Creative Directors: Dustin Cromarty, Frida Abaroa
Editors: Miriam Hick, Laurie Tissington

First edition published in book form by *Cooking with Monkey Productions Corporation* in May 2012

Buck is a part of the *Fly Me To The Moon Bubba* series.

ISBN **978-0-9878977-4-9**

Printed and bound by Hua-Ri Printing Company of Wenzhou, China
Number of prints: 5000

From the Fly me to the Moon Bubba Series

Author: Dustin Cromarty
Illustrator: Yanet Zamudio Castro
Colourist: Omar Lara Cadó
Graphic Designer: Omar Lara Cadó
Creative Directors: Dustin Cromarty, Frida Abaroa
Editors: Miriam Hick, Laurie Tissington

Cooking with Monkey©
Productions Corporation

"Tonight's tale is about a pail.
He is a big giant
known as Buck!"

"Buck carries a lot of feelings in his bucket."

"Buck takes any feeling and throws it up into the sun where it is then turned into wonderful rainbows."

One day,
Buck was sitting on a mountain
enjoying the sun, when a group of
children came up to him.

"Buck, we feel angry." they said.

"Why do you feel angry?"
asked Buck.

"We just saw a kid being bullied!"

"That's not right!" Buck protested.

"Did you help?" asked Buck.
"Yes! We said,
stop being mean!"

"And they told us to go away."
said the children.

"What?" Buck sputtered.

"They must have been from Waa Waa Ville, but at least you tried to help."

"Here, give me your angry feelings. I will throw them into the sun and it will turn them into feelings of joy."

The children frowned as they gave Buck their angry feelings.

With a big swing,
Buck threw their angry
feelings into the sun.

As the anger hit the sun it burst into flames and a dazzling rainbow shot back.

"That was amazing!"
shouted the kids jumping up and
down with joy.

"Those were beautiful fireworks!"

"Oh, wow!"
The children said staring into the sky,
watching the fireworks.

"Now, take the joy from these fireworks and do something great with it!"

"Find the boy who was being
bullied and say,
'You are not alone,'
and give him a hug."

"We will! That is a great idea!"
the children agreed.
"Thank you so much, Buck!"

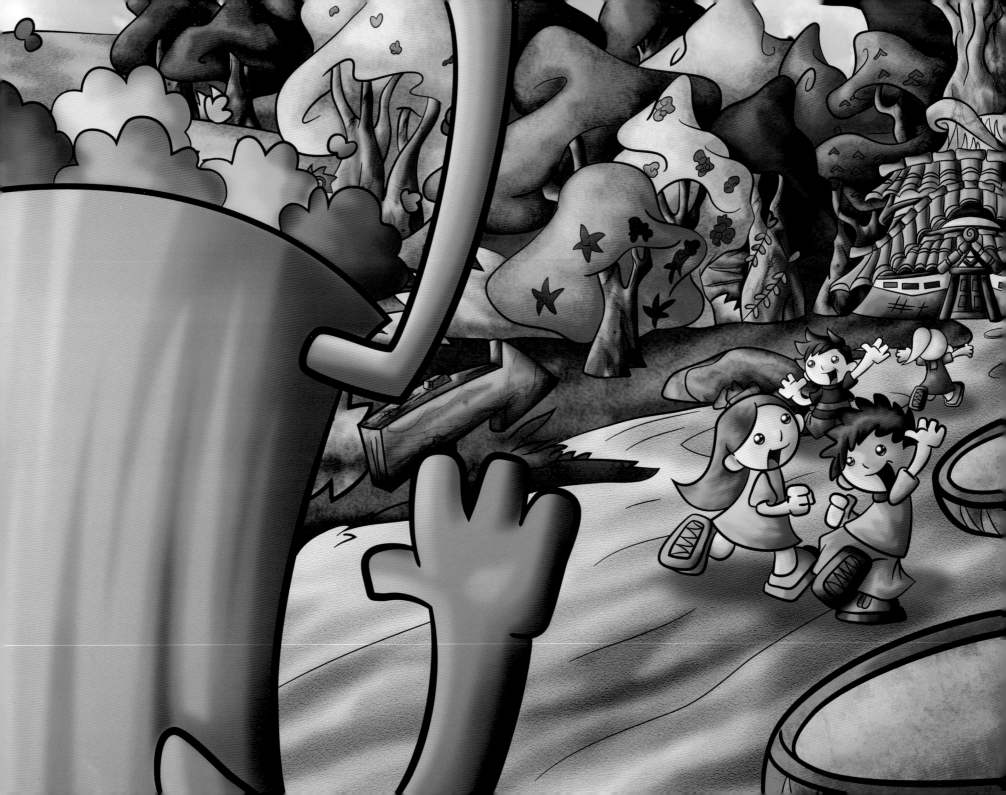

"Let's end bullying everywhere!"

"We will, Buck, we will do something wonderful!"

"In fact, the children from this story
did something wonderful.

They found the boy
who had been bullied. Together,
they made compassion snacks.
They gave them to me to share
with you tonight."

"Oh, wow! Thank you so much, Bubba!"
cheered everyone,
as they enjoyed the yummy
compassion snacks.

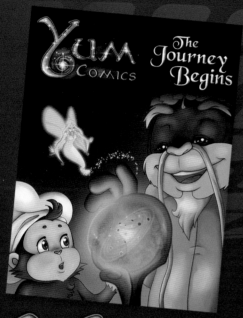